For Rosi

Seasonal Greetings!

Anthony

Brian Statham 08

Photographs

Brian Statham

Greville Press Pamphlet

First published in 2008 by The Greville Press
6 Mellors Court, The Butt, Warwick CV34 4ST

ISBN 978 0 9559151 7 8

Printed in Great Britain

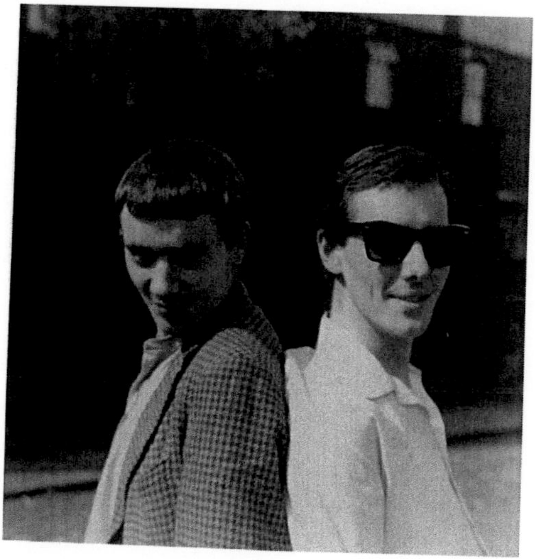

In memory of
Norman Chadwick and Robert Beardsworth

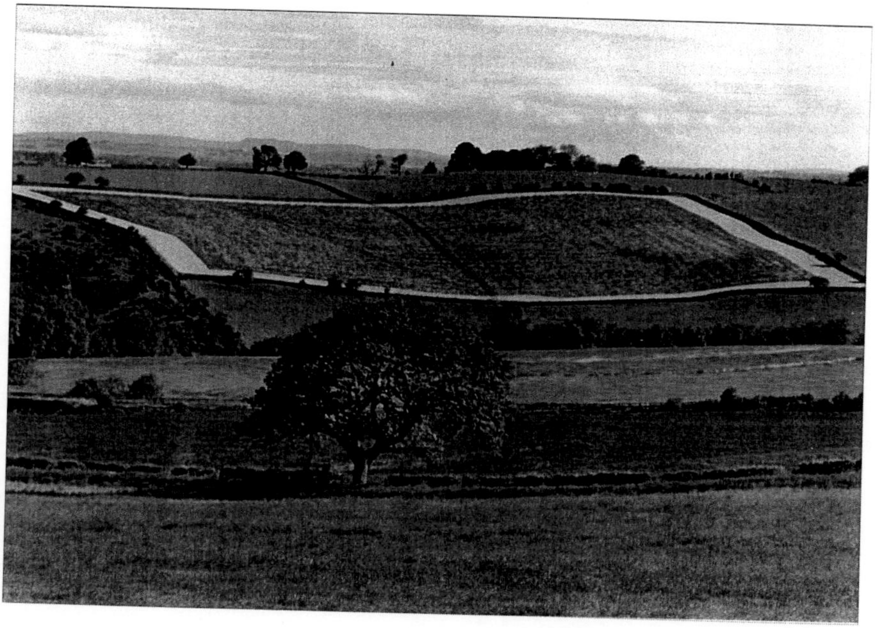

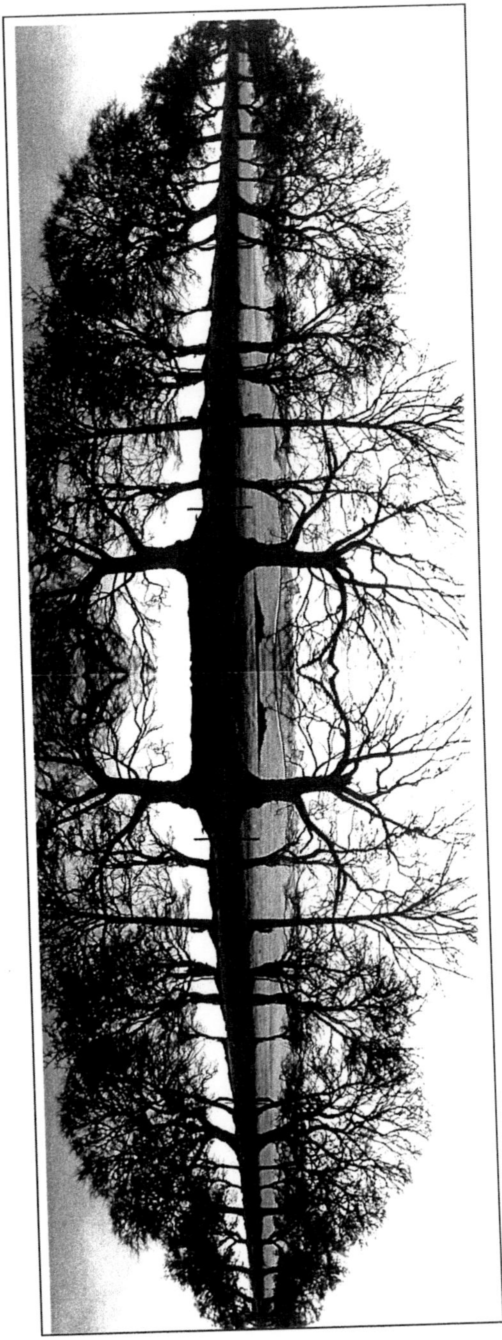

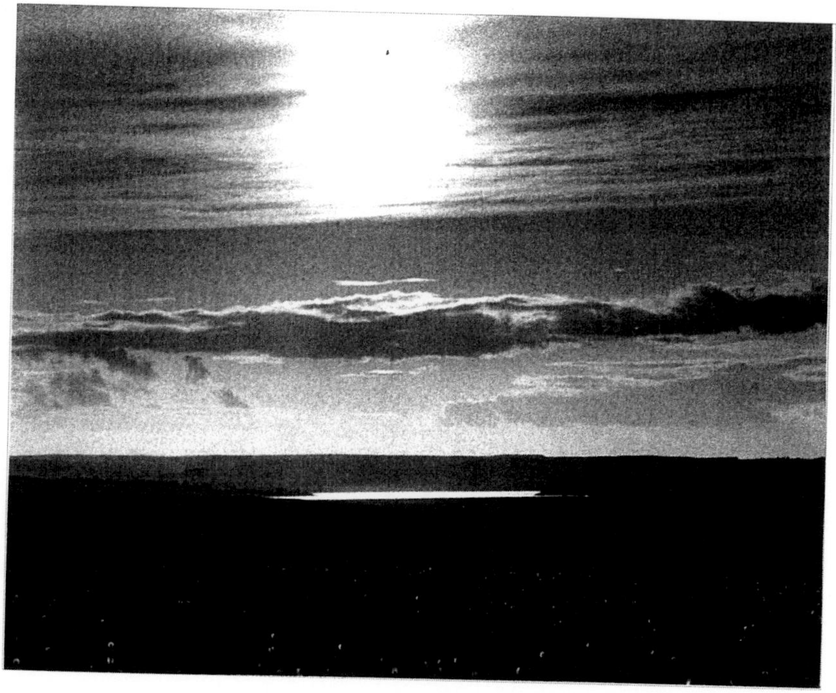

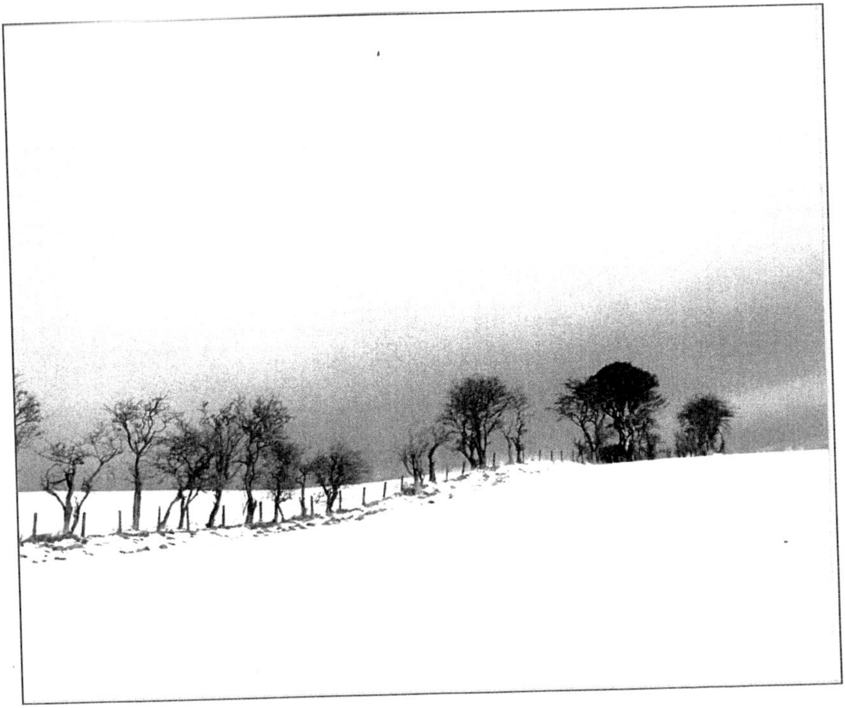

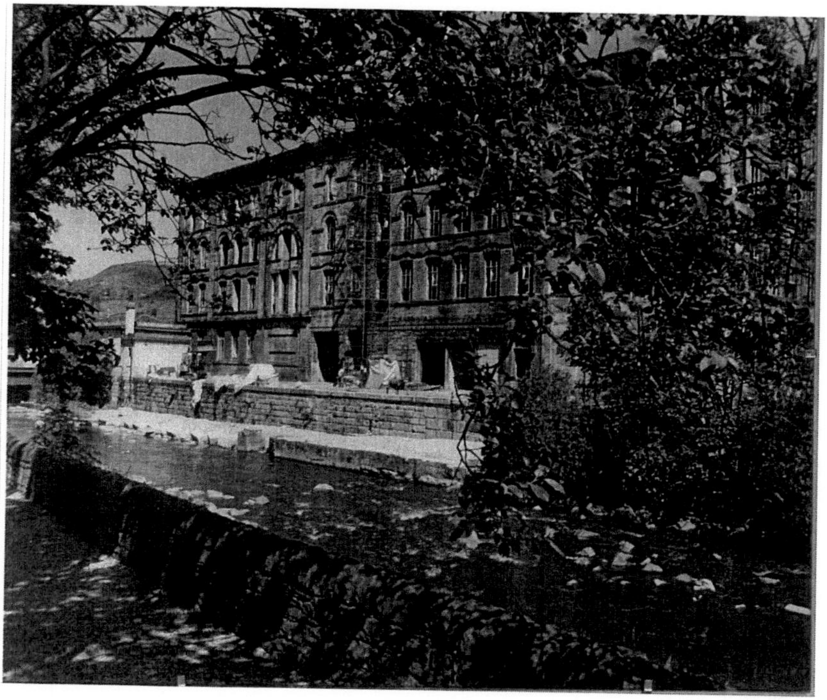

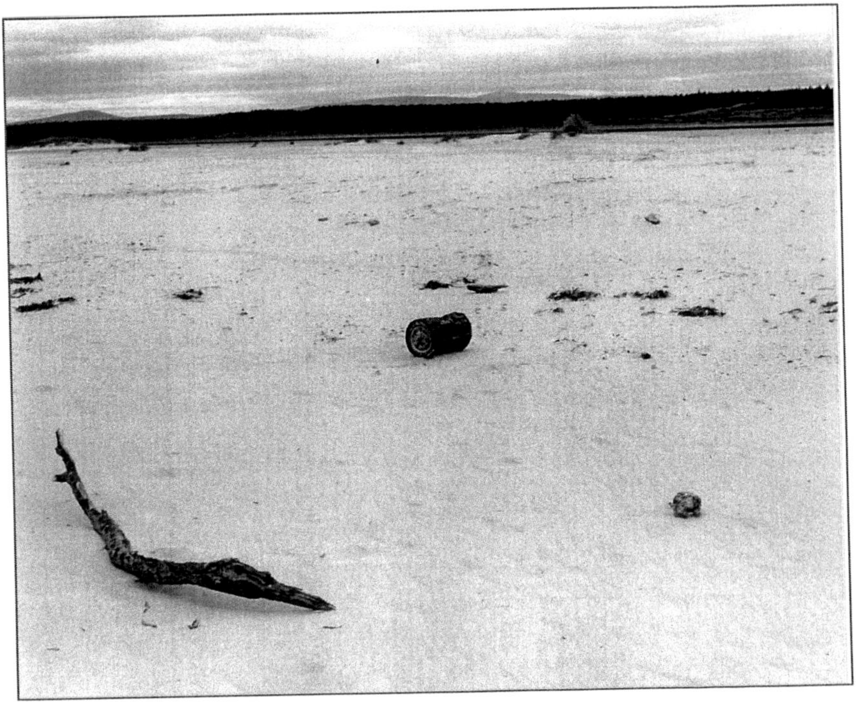

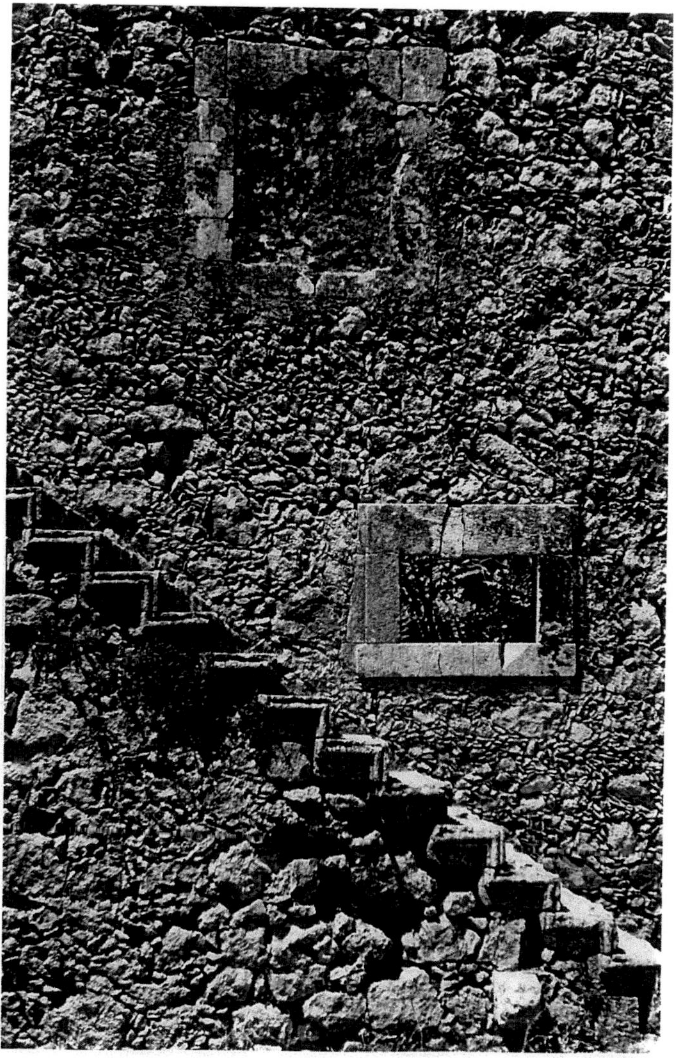

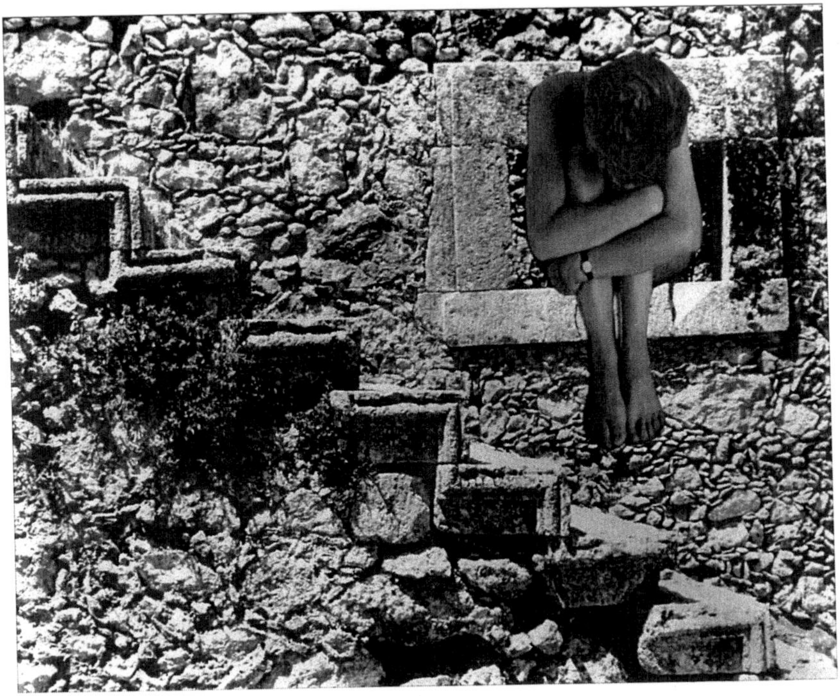

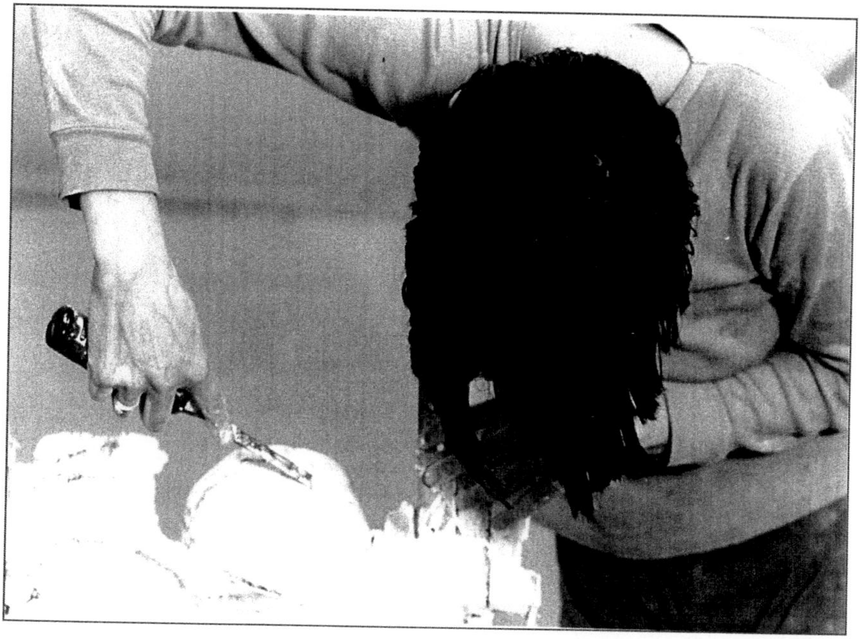

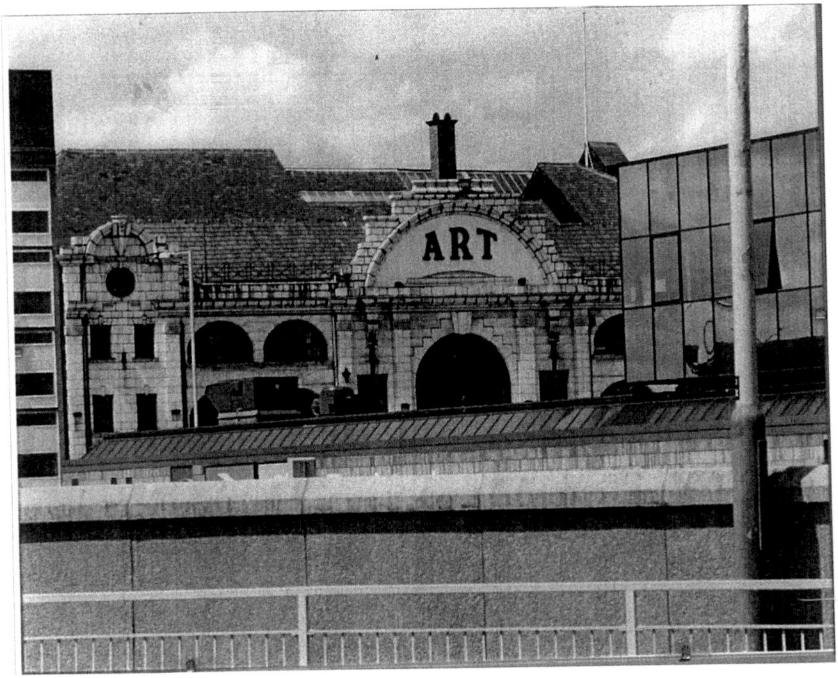
ART

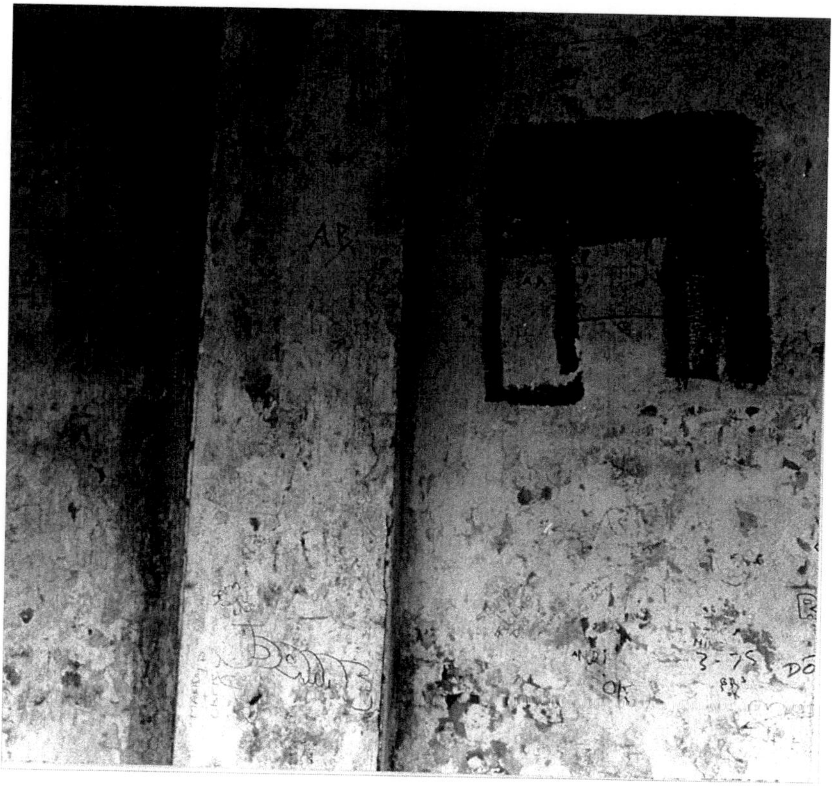

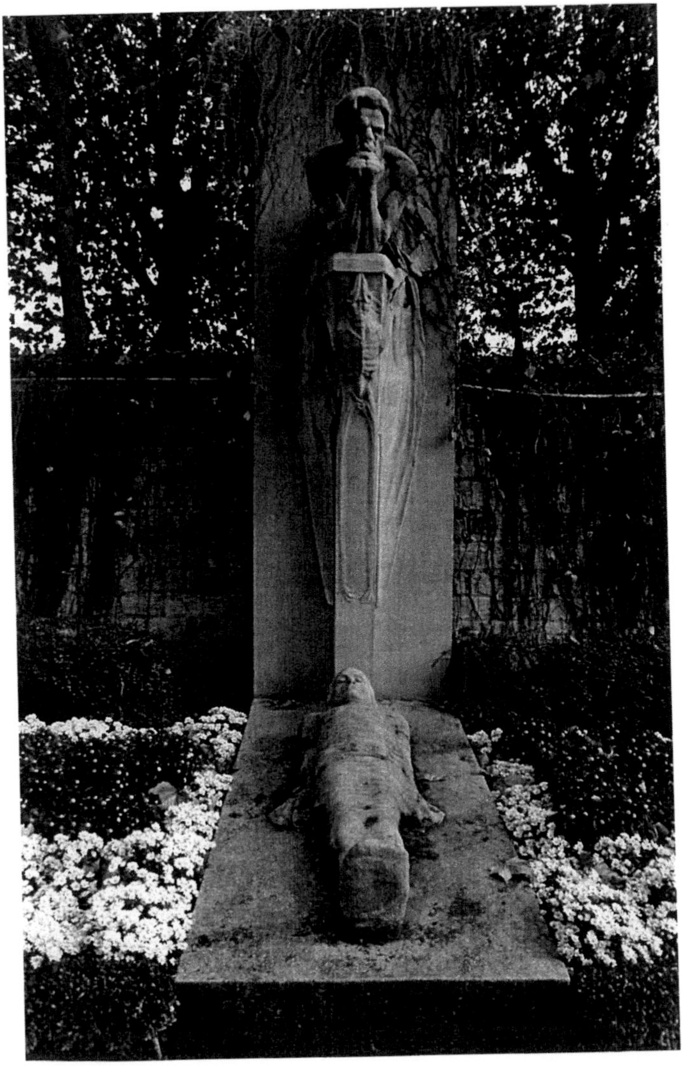